Point With Your Fingers
and Wiggle Your Toes

Sonia Maria
Illustrated by Lucy Shin

Point With Your Fingers and Wiggle Your Toes

Copyright © 2023 Sonia M Webster
All rights reserved under International and Pan-American Copyright Conventions.

No part of this publication may be reproduced, stored in a retrieval system or transmitted in any form or any means, electronic, mechanical, photocopying, recording or otherwise without the prior written permission of the copyright owner.
Contact us at roadreefpress@gmail.com
ISBN
978-1-915695-12-3 Paperback
978-1-915695-13-0 Hardcover
978-1-915695-14-7 Electronic

Library of Congress Control Number: 2022920638

Summary: Children learn basic body parts through rhymes and interactive play.
1. Stories in rhyme; 2. Concepts - Body; 3. Concepts - Counting and Numbers;
4. Concepts - Senses and Sensation; 5. Concepts – Sounds.
Printed and distributed in the United States.

For Teilyr, Elizabeth and Enzo

Love You Lots!

I have two hands that clap, clap, clap!

And on my knees they tap, tap, tap!

My hands wave

HELLO!

...And GOODBYE!
Can yours do that?
Why don't you try?

They walk and run...

...and skip in place.
They take me to my favorite space.

I have two eyes that
BLINK,
BLINK,
BLINK!

I use just one to
WINK,
WINK,
WINK!

And when I play peek-a-boo
I use them both to look at you.

My ears hear things I cannot see,
like when my **dad** sings just for me.

I hear my dog bark
WOOF,
WOOF,
WOOF!

Two hands.
Two feet.
Two eyes.
Two ears.

It seems my parts all come in pairs.

But wait! Sniff, sniff! What is that smell?

I have a nose and it can tell.

A flower, my lunch, or a stinky shoe?
    SNIFF,
        SNIFF!

I have one nose, not two!

Below my nose I have a mouth.
Hurray! Hurray! I like to shout.

I use my mouth to eat and sing
and call my **Mom** for everything!

I have ten fingers that I use,
to count and point...

...and tie my shoes.

Inside my shoes are ten little toes.
I can wiggle, wiggle mine.
Can you wiggle, wiggle yours?

There are many other parts of me,
like shoulders, elbows, arms, and knees.
And when I run and dance and play,
it's always an amazing day.

Then when the night is drawing near,
I stretch and yawn from ear to ear.

I rest my head to dreams so sweet.
Tomorrow is another treat.

www.ingramcontent.com/pod-product-compliance
Lightning Source LLC
Chambersburg PA
CBHW041800290426
43661CB00132B/1237